Here We Go

words and paintings

Debra Briggs Whiteflower

Here We Go: Words and Paintings
Published by Debra Whiteflower

ISBN: 979-8-218-74225-6 (paperback)

ART / Individual Artists / Artists' Books

POETRY / General

Illustrations and Design Credits

All artwork © Debra Whiteflower.
Cover design by Amanda Miller; cover artwork © Debra Whiteflower.
Interior design by Asya Blue; design copyright © Debra Whiteflower.

For author or book-related inquiries, please email:debrawhiteflower@gmail.com

Dedicated to my beloved children,
grandchildren, family and friends

as well as
to
World Peace

May All Beings Be Happy

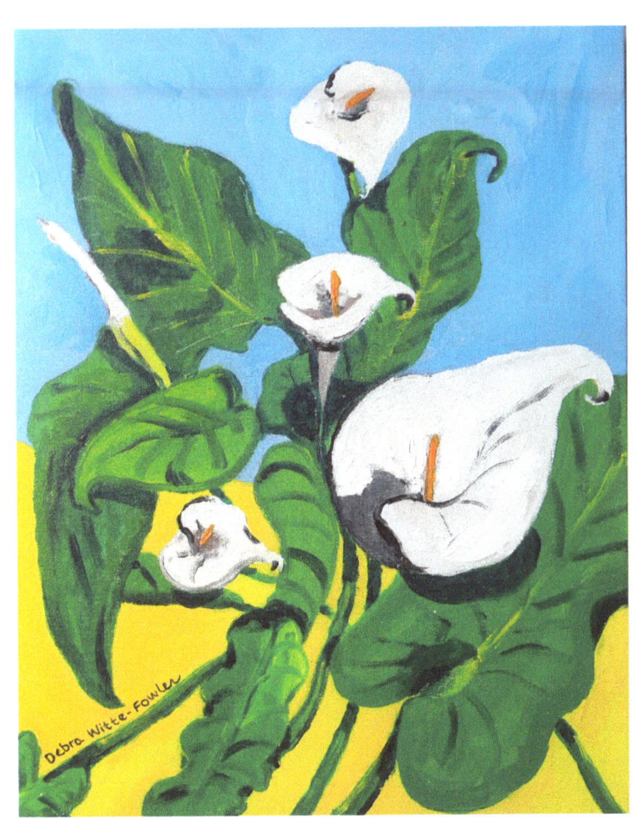

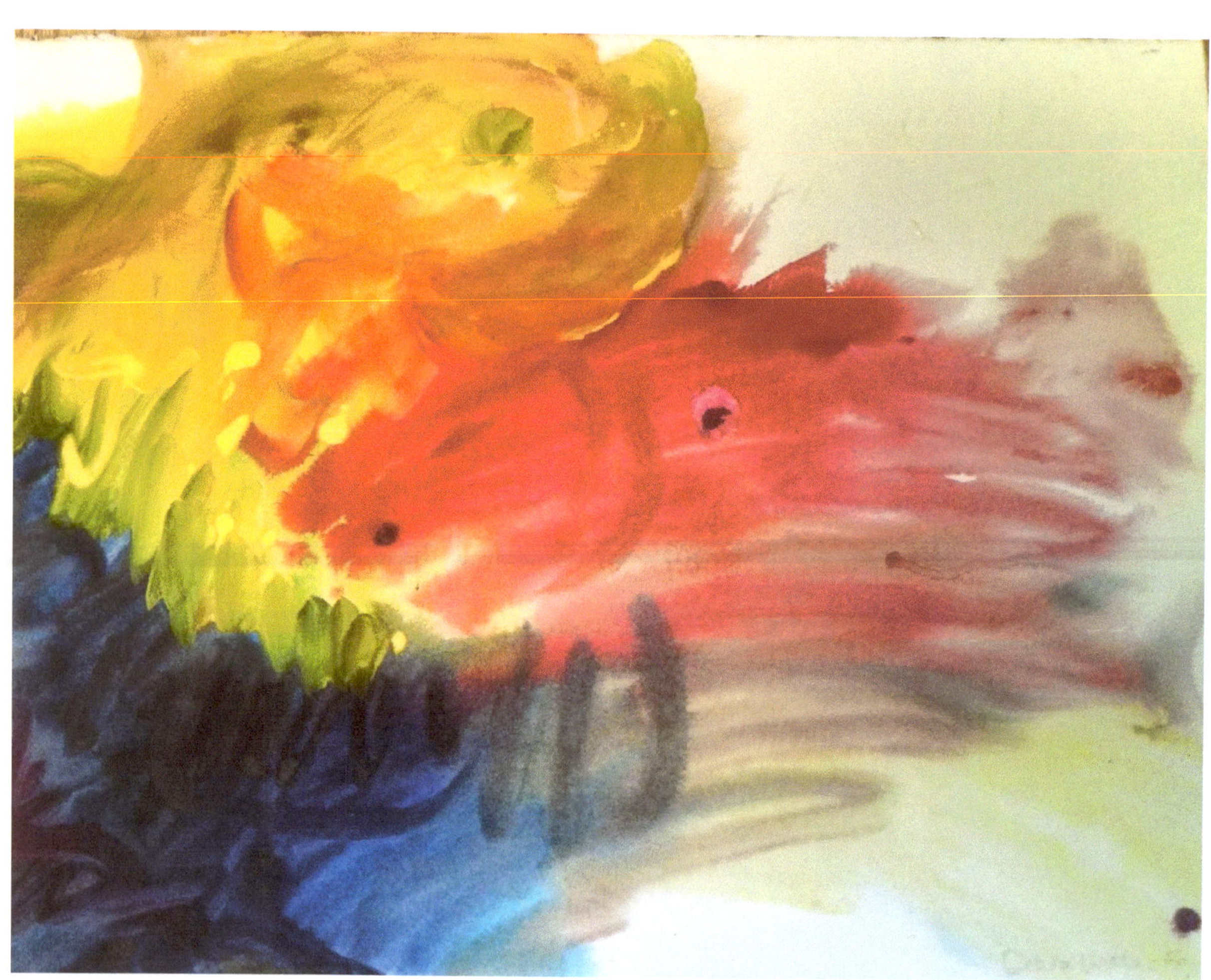

My Wild Horse Mind

My mind is a wild horse
charging
She wants free rein
at times thirsting
for anger
for fear
for thrills

that leave me empty

True slaking,
my gut knows,
comes cool at the
river
within

But gallop she will, that mind of mine
chanting,
HE DID THIS, SHE SAID THAT

"Let it go," I cry,
tugging on the reins

"Be mindful, pay attention.
What do you love?
The past?
Old hurts?
Stress?"

I pull hard on my
running wild thoughts
"Wake up," I call
"Know your own heart.
What satisfies?"

Peace of mind
Joyful heart

So I stroke and calm my
wild horse mind
take her for a deep drink
at the inner river and make friends
with my horse heart,

my wild horse mind

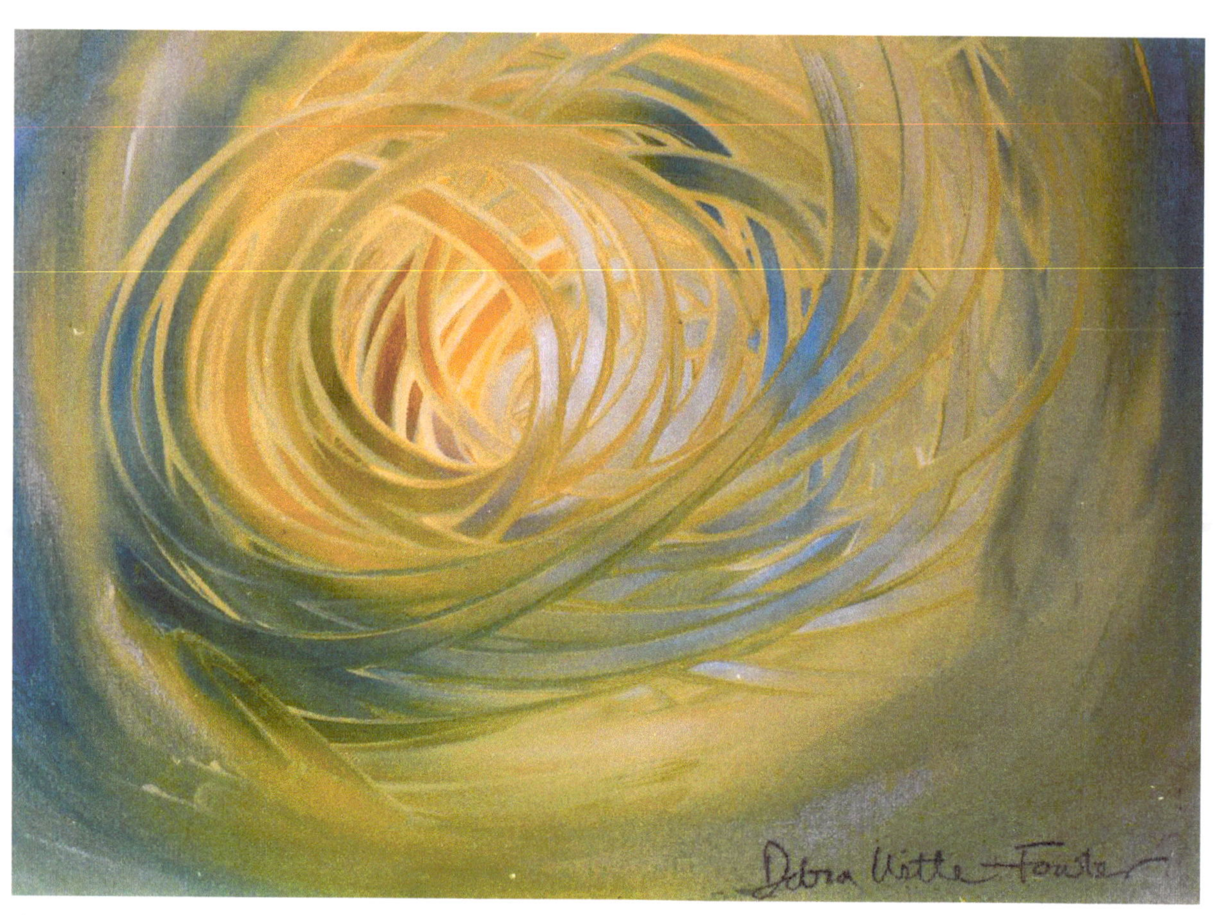

Solo Contento

My house is falling apart
The one I've been putting together with another
For fifteen years
I'm forgetting how to breathe

Not yet ready to walk out
I escape
for a few days
with a friend's borrowed truck

Gray Sunday
no particular place to be
I pull off the road
scruffy grass, crunchy lava
I face into mountains
I cannot see

Deflated with fatigue,
grief, dead-end loneliness, I sit

Five years later . . .
Coming home from a few hours of dancing
with friends, acquaintances,
no particular partner,
the moon follows me over my shoulder
as I pull into the spot

same scruffy grass, lava crunch under the tires
facing what I now know are the slopes
of Mauna Loa and Manua Kea,
though the night's too dark to see

Wind whips blowing mist past my car,
night phantoms, dancing,
music pulsing from pandora
I sit alert
glued to the vast now and thrill
of ecstatic solitude

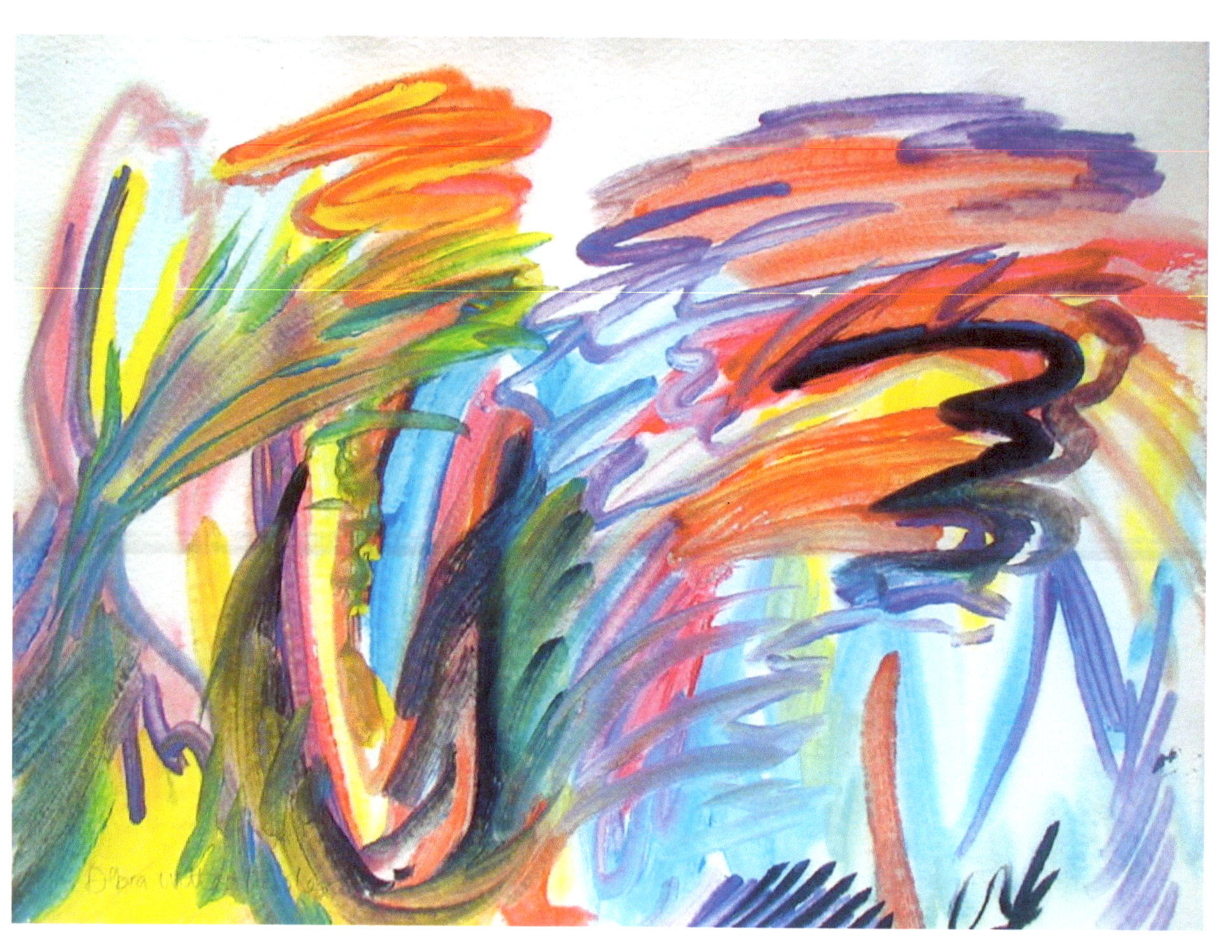

Words

Words
my own,
other's
written,
spoken
fail me now

In a space of unknowing
words say
"I know."
and I don't

I'm in between
words

Words want to contain
but how to contain
questions?
magic?
loss?
change?

How can words
hold the meaning
of sticky, green
emergence

How do words describe
grief that empties
a gut?

How can words,
so solid on paper
or holding space
in time,
capture the rush of cold
streamwaters
on hot, tired flesh
the momentary release
of pain
into skin-numbing water
pop
and spark?

Words want to mean something

How can
what is changing in an instant
be captured?

How is *transformation*
even a word?

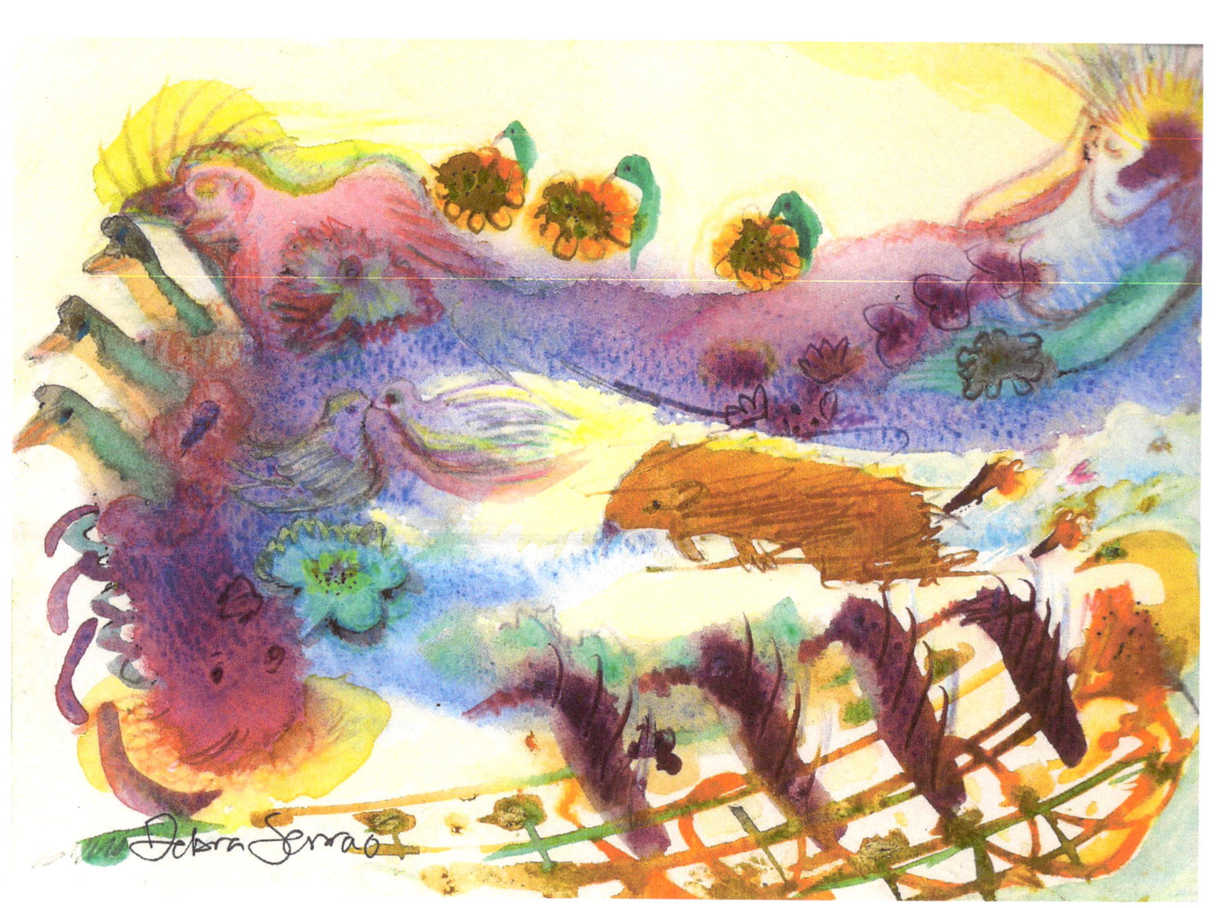
Debra Serrao

Wood Valley in the Rain

Celebrating 76
with a walk in the rain
a slight drizzle
but I have my umbrella
the one that's rainbow colors

The air, filled with mist and green
as I stroll down the road

Up ahead a young steer by a fence

Even as I approach
he continues to chew his cud
and swish his tail
not moving from his spot

I am a passing image to him
I'm fine with that
So apparently, is he

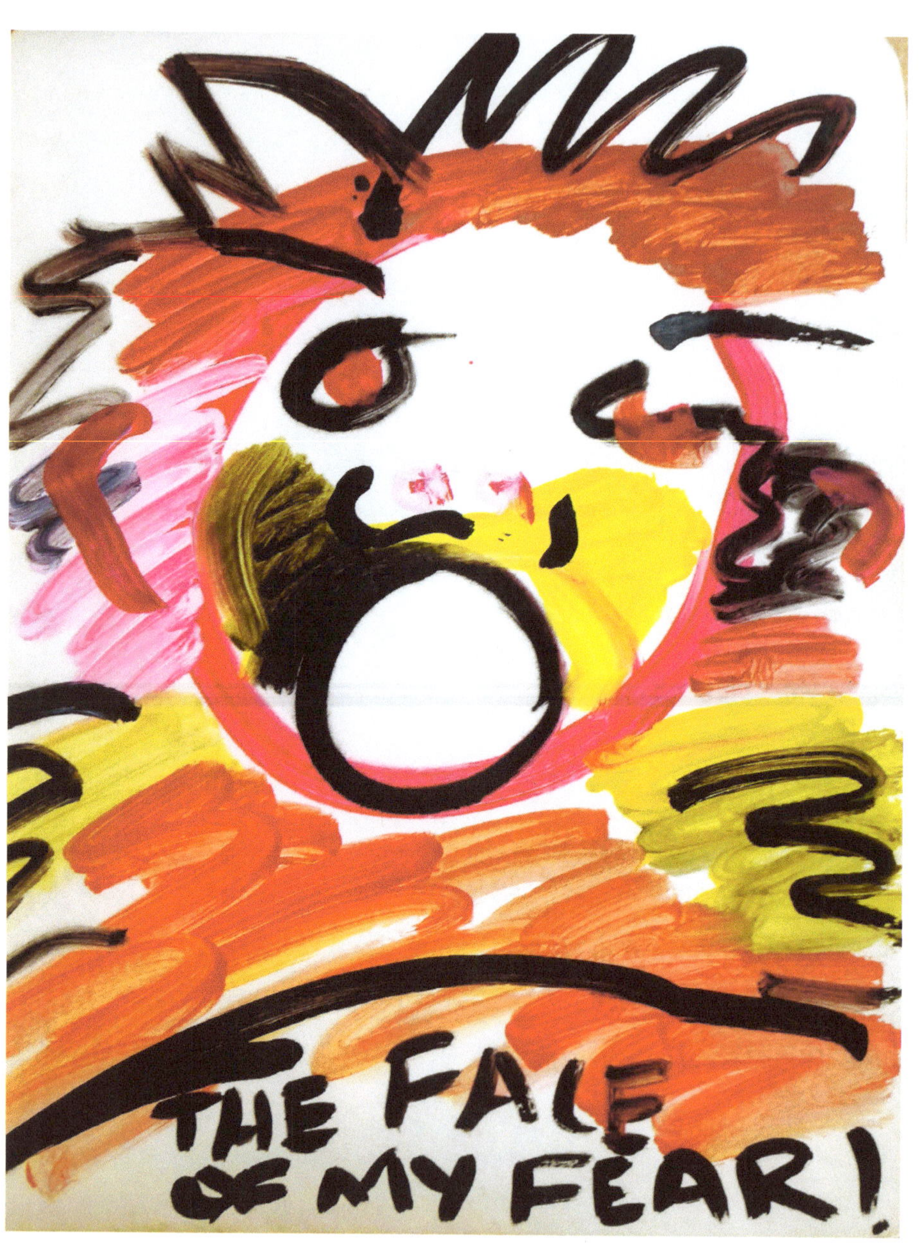
THE FACE
OF MY FEAR!

Don Juan and Carlos

I'm getting it more and more

When Don Juan told Carlos to sit and be still for a spell
Oh, and notice, he pointed out,
that coyote out there on the desert, but don't be bothered by him
The coyote that later turned out
to be a branch and a rock, that from
that certain angle and late-day light only *resembled* a coyote

Was the lesson for ALL of us --
    all the imagined coyotes or poisonous snakes
are each a thought?
in our minds?

The coyote-thought, planted by Don Juan,
the thought that threatened to freak out Castaneda while he tried to sit calmly in the desert,
is like our misconceptions, judgments, fears

When we take a closer look
they may be only a rock and a tree branch,
not the scary thing we first imagine

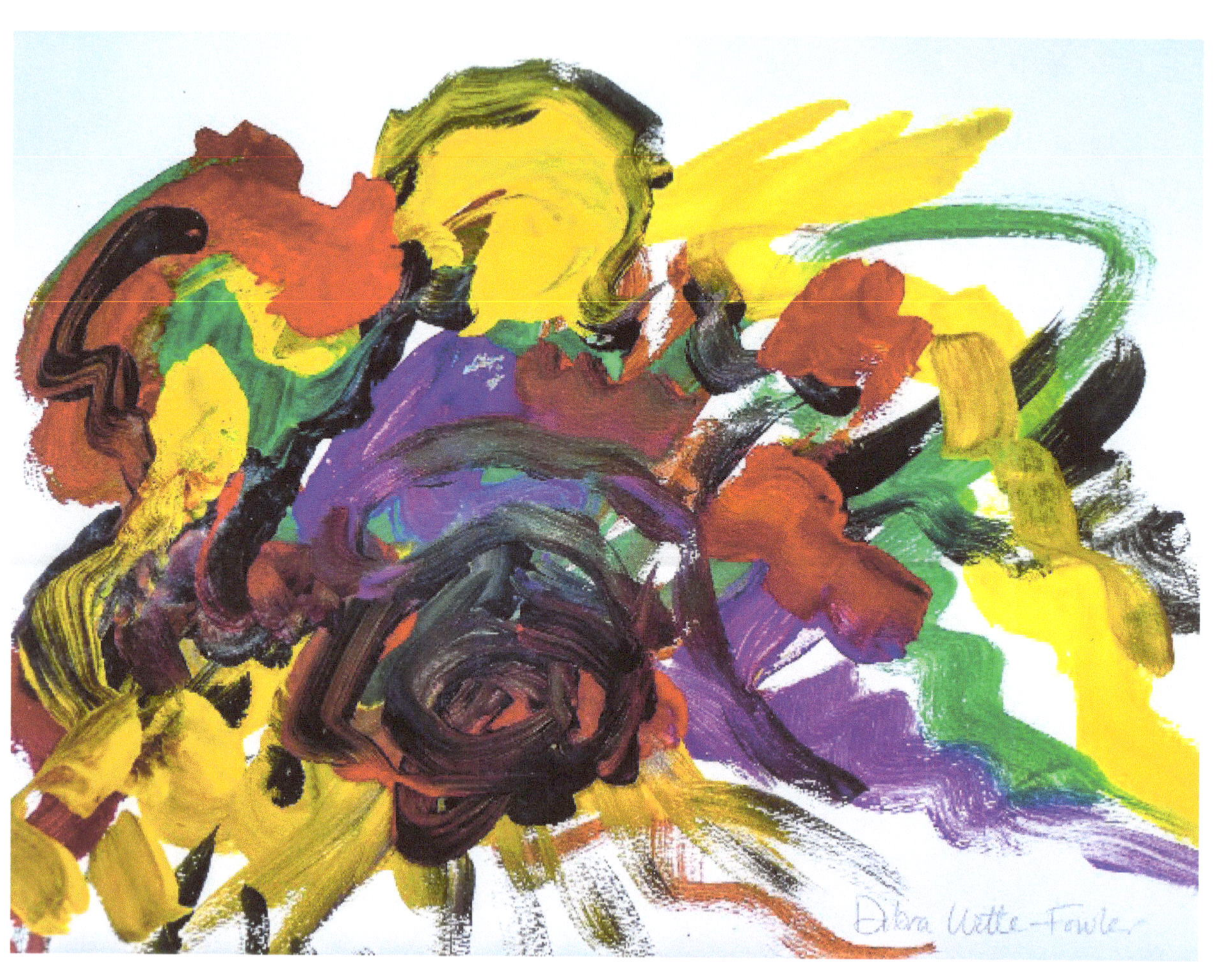
Debra Witte-Fowler

Stumped

Lately I'm stumped by life
I do one thing and
then I want to sit
or eat, or drink something sweet
Then go perch again
struggling to focus
I surrender to inaction

But then the sun comes out
and suddenly I want to take a walk

Heading to my post office box
I pass a small box of trash
that hasn't moved in weeks

On my way back home I use
a plastic bag I
carry with me,
use it like a glove, pick up the
rain-softened box

In a block or two
the several discarded beer bottles
and other trash in the box,
prove heavier than I thought
Trash left behind by some workers
from a nearby jobsite,
I surmise

I'd like to scold them,
be their Mother, remind them
they could do better
We could all do better

I set the box down
every block or so
giving a rest to my right thumb that's
doing the work

At the corner where I turn
towards home, I set the box down again
and look to the sky
a blue, breezy sky with a myriad of small clouds
covering the expanse

And there he is
an 'Io, Hawaiian hawk,
and I call "Hey, 'Io"
and I call and call
as he sails and circles high, high, higher
away and then back again
And the light shines just right
and I see his whole
underbelly, golden
and his wings spread wide
"'Io,' Io" I call
Renewed

I needed a sunny day
I needed an 'Io
I needed an unexpected call from my son
I needed a day to be stumped

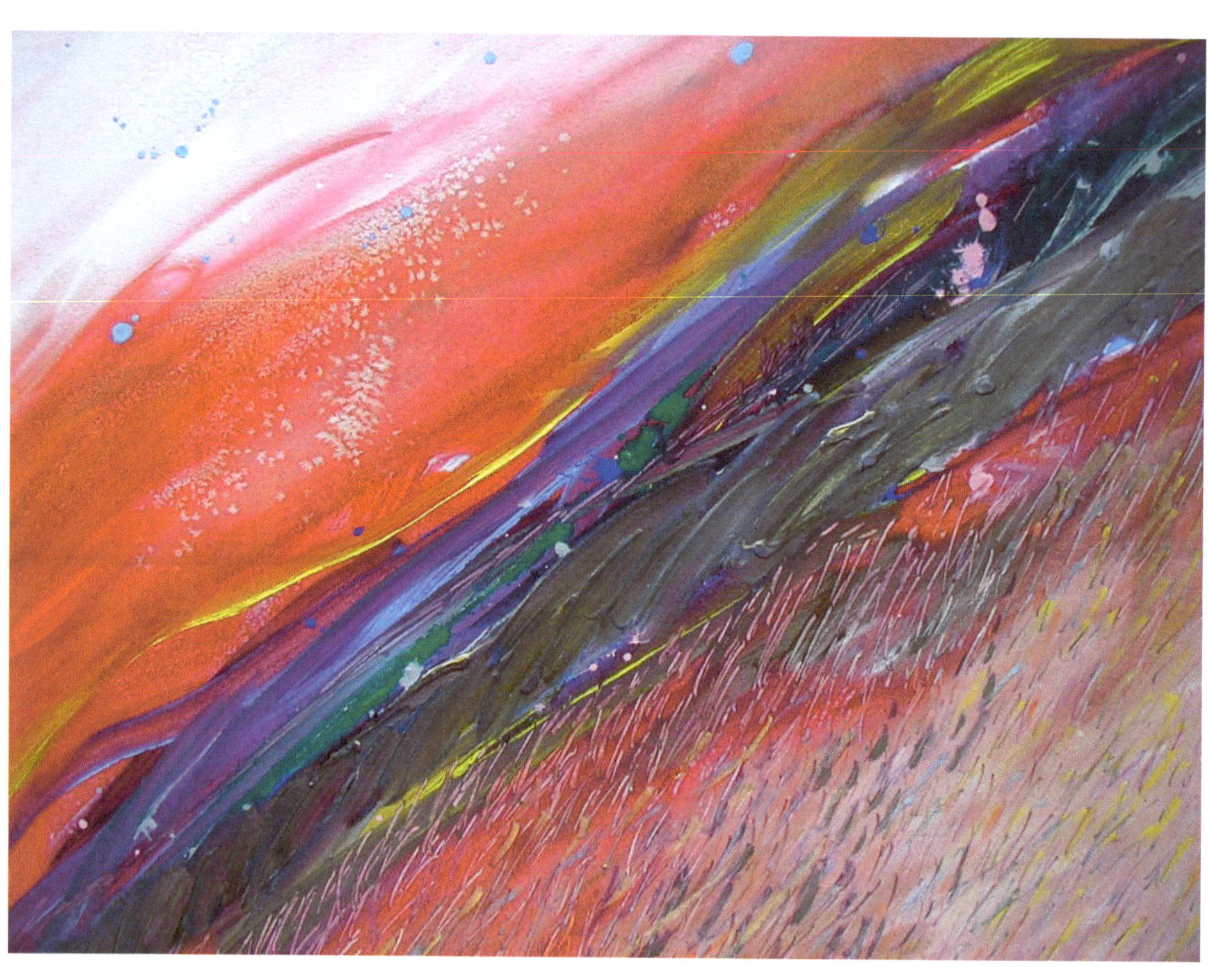

It Takes a Volcano

It takes a volcano erupting under our island to stir us all. Like a delicate web stretched over the whole of our Big Island, Hawai'i, we are all feeling the vibration, in varying degrees, of her, Madame Pele's, emergence.

Beginning in sea level in the Puna district with quakes, tremors and cracks in the road, to gasses coming up between those widening cracks to jets of lava to *fountains* of lava, moving into yards, bumping up against houses, devouring those homes or moving on. Soon we were giving number names to those fissures as new ones emerged.

She has moved from giant plumes of lava (the biggest named Fissure 8), into a huge "River of Lava" rushing faster than we can run, pouring through forest, orchards, farmland, more homes. With the dropping of the lava lake from our Kilauea Crater, the earth began to shake and quake at 4,000 feet. Our geologists tell us that the lava moving underground (they are not even sure of the exact course), keeps flowing down, down to the ocean, emerging from the earth, gushing, roaring to demolish land that's been loved and will no longer be seen in order to create new land.

We are at more than 3 months of the new now. Some have lost homes, property, livelihoods, some have lost fresh air to breathe. Ash has rained down, the ground shook us out of our dreams into the truth of impermanence. All things change. New life comes from death and destruction. New seeds are released. All can become new.

It takes a volcano to learn to let go of what we knew was true, to open us to all that is possible.

Letter to the Editor, *Hilo Tribune*, 2018

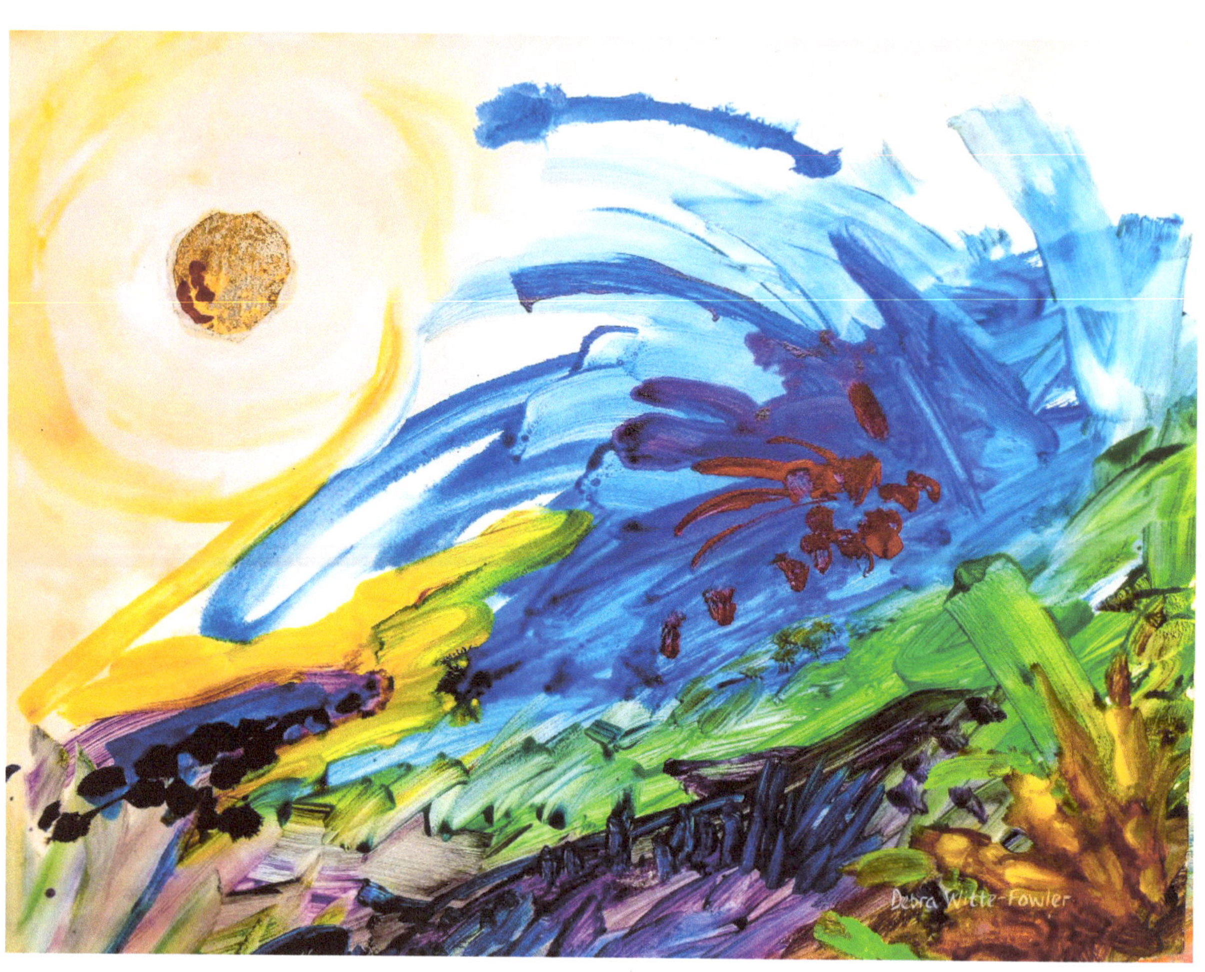
Debra Witte-Fowler

The Children's Laughter

His name is well-known
One of the first westerners ordained as a Buddhist monk

He was speaking at one of my favorite places on the
island, a small temple in Wood Valley
45 minutes from my house

I arrived early,
found an easy place to park and walked
up the hill to the temple
From the doorway I could see it was
filled with maroon cushions affixed with
green labels that read "Staff"

Folding chairs encircled the veranda,
some with tags, some unnamed
I chose an empty seat near an open window
and waited quietly while others arrived,
gathering in small groups to visit
or finding their designated cushions or chairs

A gong wrang, folks quieted
and then our guest was introduced
I settled into my chair comfortably,
relaxed, opened my ears and waited

When he spoke it was difficult to hear his
every word, I knew I was not the only one,
most of us were seated outside the small
temple space
Our distinguished speaker is an author and a
storyteller
The rise and fall of his voice was
joined by intermittent laughter
coming mostly from inside

Sometimes I caught the words and the joke,
but the warm sun on my shoulders was
welcomed after days of wind and rain

Children's voices, carried by a breeze,
threatened to overpower the stream of the speaker's voice

What a bother, one of my inner voices said,
Shouldn't the parents do something?
And then, a calmer inner voice said
Let their voices be, let their soft laughter be part
of what there is to hear

I took a breath and noticed how soothing
was the recent paint job on the temple,
the bright yellow a lovely balance to the soft
melon orange,
the creamy gray of the floor boards, smooth and
inviting to bare feet

The speaker is reminding us that emptiness
is not empty space
Emptiness is everything, all together,
and is the truth

The dharma talk, the children's laughter, the
wind, the sun, the bodies to the right and the left
Have I come for a speech?
Have I come to hear a famous Buddhist string words
together?
Or have I come for an experience of bliss and emptiness

When the time for questions comes
I stay for the first question,
a long-winded one from a wordy man
who kept interrupting our honored guest
by telling him he wasn't done with his question yet
I waited,
in case I might miss some wisdom.

I stayed through the famous-one's rebuttal
to the long-winded question
and then gathered my things and quietly departed
as the next questioner, a male, took the floor

Time to go, it was clear

If I had truly come for enlightenment
I had better go before it quickly dissipated

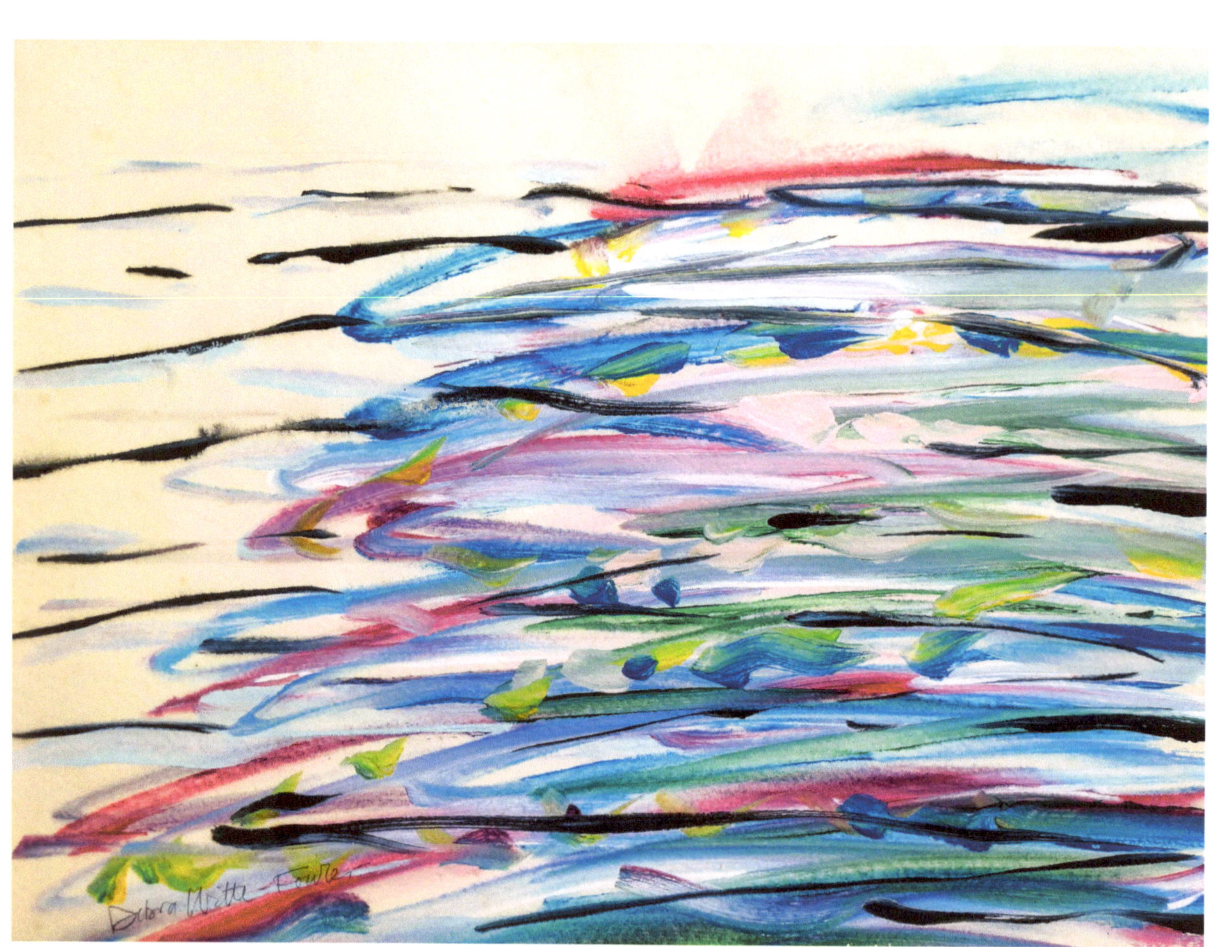

Maya, Our Dance of Delusion

So maybe, Friends,
the lesson is to look beyond our drama stories

We are in school, earth school: the lessons, the hard,
the terrible, painful, gut-wrenching lessons of loss, of
heartbreak, of illness, of decay, all nudge us to look
deeper, to strip
the layers of our most tender parts

Gutted, flayed,
is it only then we might remember
we are not our bodies?
We are consciousness, spirit, energy particles, mind,
not our bodies

Living feels HARDER towards the end
Wait, what? We thought we'd bypass death and dying?
We wouldn't age? That part would not happen for us?
Joints wear out, organs malfunction,
hearing, vision, so much is lost
We just don't expect it to happen to us
Are we so stubborn the only way we remember we are
more than our body
is by watching it disintegrate?

Perhaps each encroaching loss is a call to
"Wake up, get busy, work on the inner
lessons, the strengths that really matter."

While we cling to the body are we just
wasting precious time when we could be
fine-tuning our inner awareness?

I'd like to wake up before I die
I'd like to remember I can choose peace, instead of fear

What would it be like to willingly walk in the muddy
boots of another
with true compassion?
Letting go of attachment
to people, to the outcomes the ego desires
Is that the path to Nirvana, Heaven, the Buddhaland?

I'm greedy to reach that now
or if not now, then as I'm dying
may I realize it's time to melt
into everything, to let go

But why is it so hard?
Why am I so blind?

Oh, but Maya, the dazzling illusion of life,
so beguiling

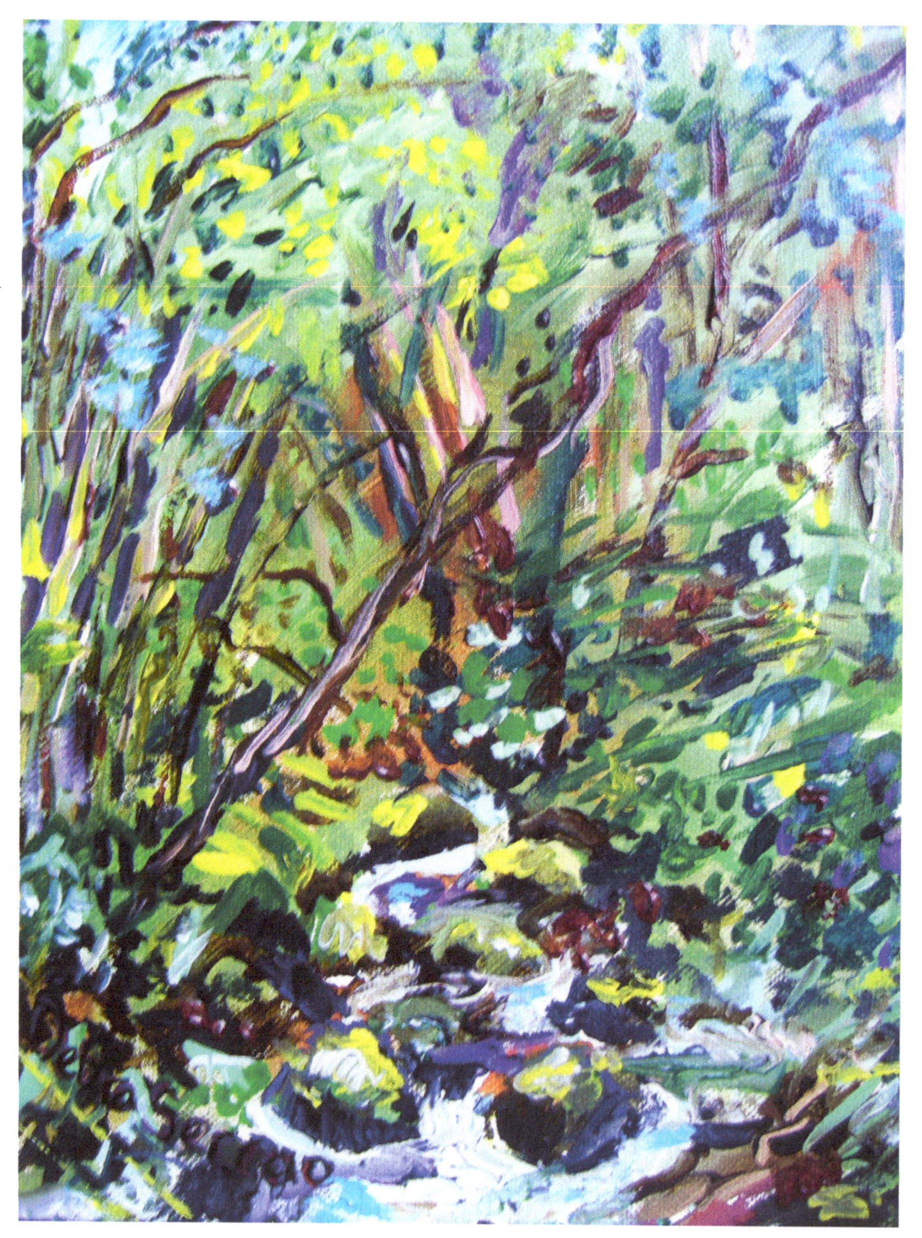

Along the Path

The guide suggests
I close my eyes
Visualize a place of beauty and peace

But I can't help but open them
for I am in a mountain forest of koa and
'ohi'a

Caught by a small movement,
my eyes follow a tiny shadow creature
making its way
along a shadow branch

"Kindness,"
I am reminded by the teacher.
There can be so much kindness.
I am always in a circle of family,
friends and wise ones,
if I but remember

What kindness
to myself and others
when I let go of clinging
to the reality I normally see
and through inner eyes
I take in the Emptiness
of vast Space and Time
and let it melt with Bliss

Emptiness and Bliss
The Pure Land
of Guides and Saints,
invisible

until I look hard
"But no strain," my teacher says.
"Look with joy and ease."

Heading home
a pair of yellow finches
I whistle to
pause to peck at the ground
then fly ahead
to land again and again
leading me up the path
to home

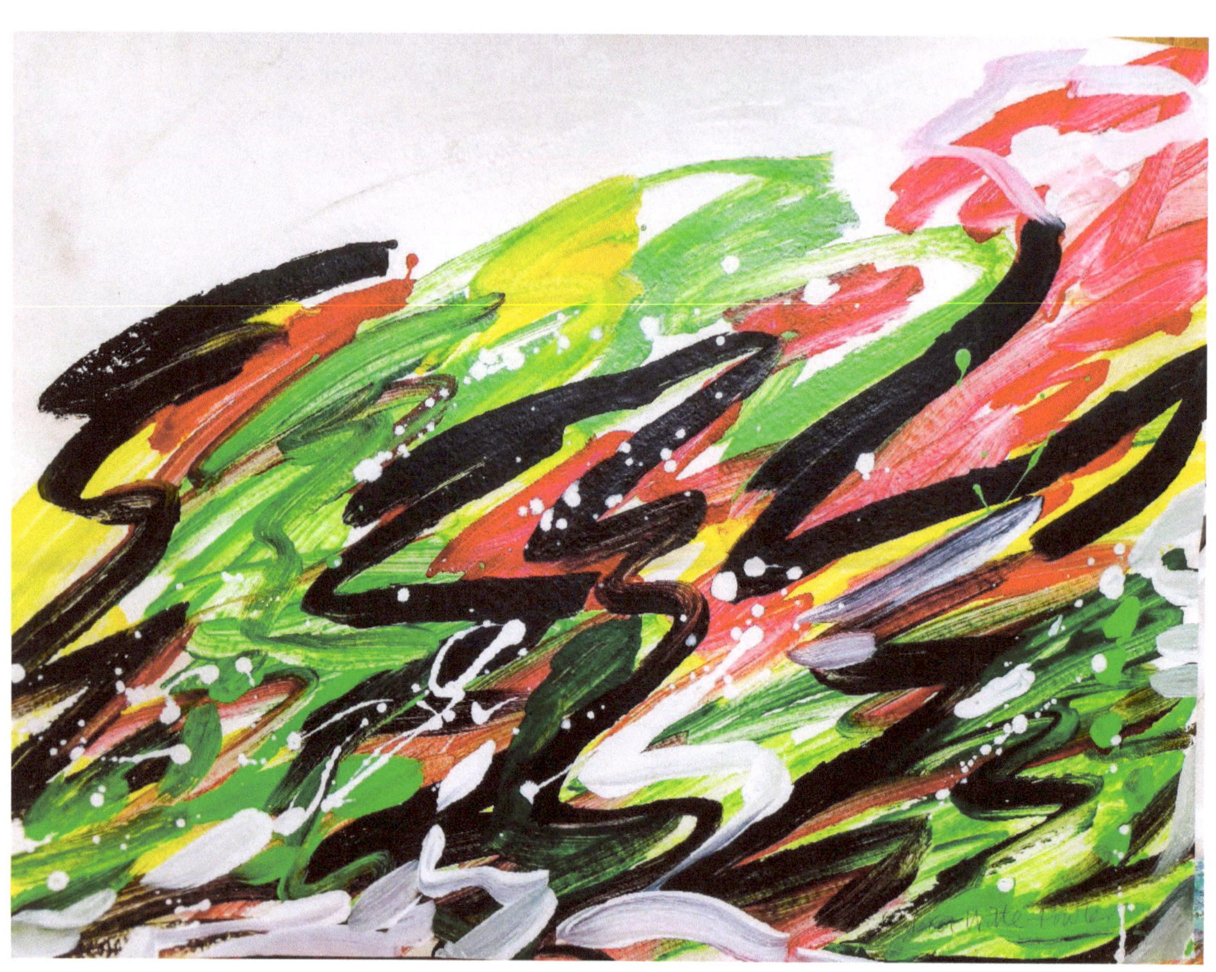

December in Volcano

A friend visits from the warm, sunny side of the island
Outside a wind and rainstorm swirls around
and over us,
while three feet of snow accumulate on the
Mauna Kea summit

We, longtime friends,
under the same blanket on opposite sides of the
window seat, cozy from the gas fireplace
that warmed us this morning,
before the power went out

Friends over 32 years
we have taken our turns
being the comforter and the comforted

Break-ups, family and marriage troubles,
agonizing heartaches
Sharing in turn the wisdoms
we each forget
when our own tsunamis toss us down

The first hug of the weekend touched off
a gush of tears
This time it is her heart that's crying
Two hits to the gut, a romance break-up
and a grown daughter rejection

These storm-filled days
are a sharing of tears and painful stories,
as together we pull from the heart-wreckage
possible lessons, new directions, responses

All boiling down, perhaps, to that universal desire --
what we all, young and old, rich and poor, strong and
weak, most yearn for
– a place to feel safe and cared for

The times after time that our hearts are wrung,
rejected, pain-riddled, bereft,
can we finally, finally see --
it is up to us?
Not the lover, the child, the friend, no one
outside ourselves

It is up to us
to create the safe and loving place
to hold firm with fragile, but unshakable certainty,
that precious, welcoming place within ourselves
where we reside and survive with gratitude

That place? -- the heart
at home, with itself.

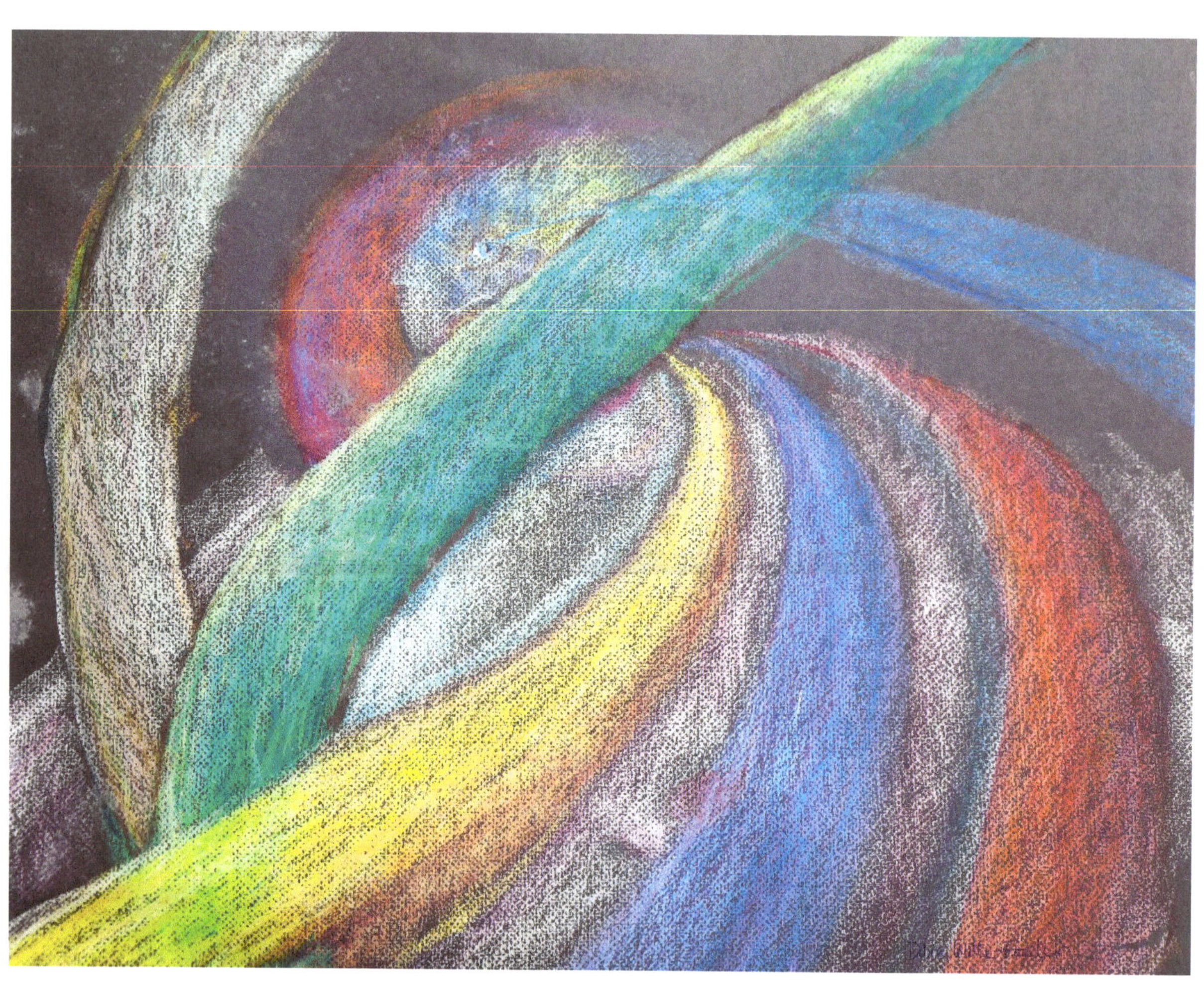

What to Do

What to do?
in the face of all that is wrong with the world
when the Ukrainian,
the Palestinian people and all other innocents
are being attacked

We are outraged, heartbroken, grief-stricken
It is our nature to suffer when others suffer
They are us

"*What is the best thing to do?*"
the spiritual teacher asks
(It's a new world when wise counsel
comes via Zoom)

What is our response when we see the pictures?
hear the stories?
read the headlines?
Will a mind of fear, anger and worry help?
Not when those are the very thoughts that foster war

What do we need to do?

Have a mind of love, the wise ones say,
Stay steady, never waver
Call upon all the STRENGTH of the higher beings:
Buddha, Jesus, Tara, Kuan Yin, the Ancestors
Ask them to change hearts,
to lift delusion from aggressors,
to give wisdom to those who can make a difference

The time is now
We are here for this
We can make a difference

What can we do?
Be in our RIGHT mind, constantly
No fear, no hate
Only love and peace
Vigilantly
Daily
Each minute
A peaceful mind of love
is what we can do

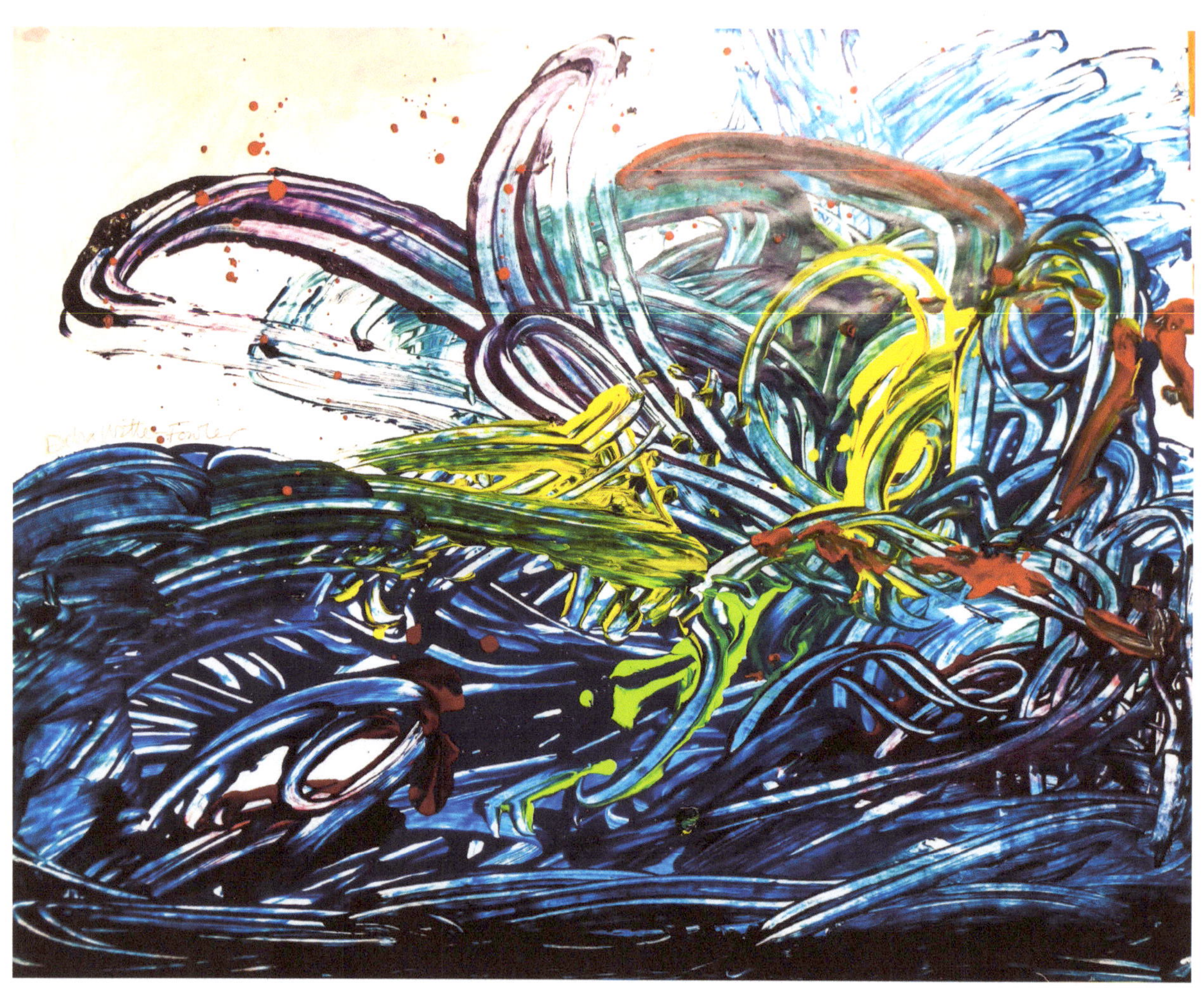

Since I Saw You Last

A deeply growing awareness that I have all I need
That "It (whatever 'IT' is) is all a Gift"

That I'm having my most profound insights and loving awarenesses
by myself
at home

It's all inside
so why go elsewhere

Nature nurtures
My own backyard is an amazing place to open my eyes
Trees, birds, sky

The' Io hawk that flies over my head
The view of snow-covered Mauna Kea from the end of the drive

Closing my eyes and seeing on the inside of my eyelids the
"other" reality of color and energy, like an Impressionist image,
that is possible, that is real

"Let possibilities happen," I am hearing. Don't be in a rush.

Don't even be in a rush to do the dishes. Slow down. Enjoy it.

Savor it all.

Oh, if I could.
Everyday.

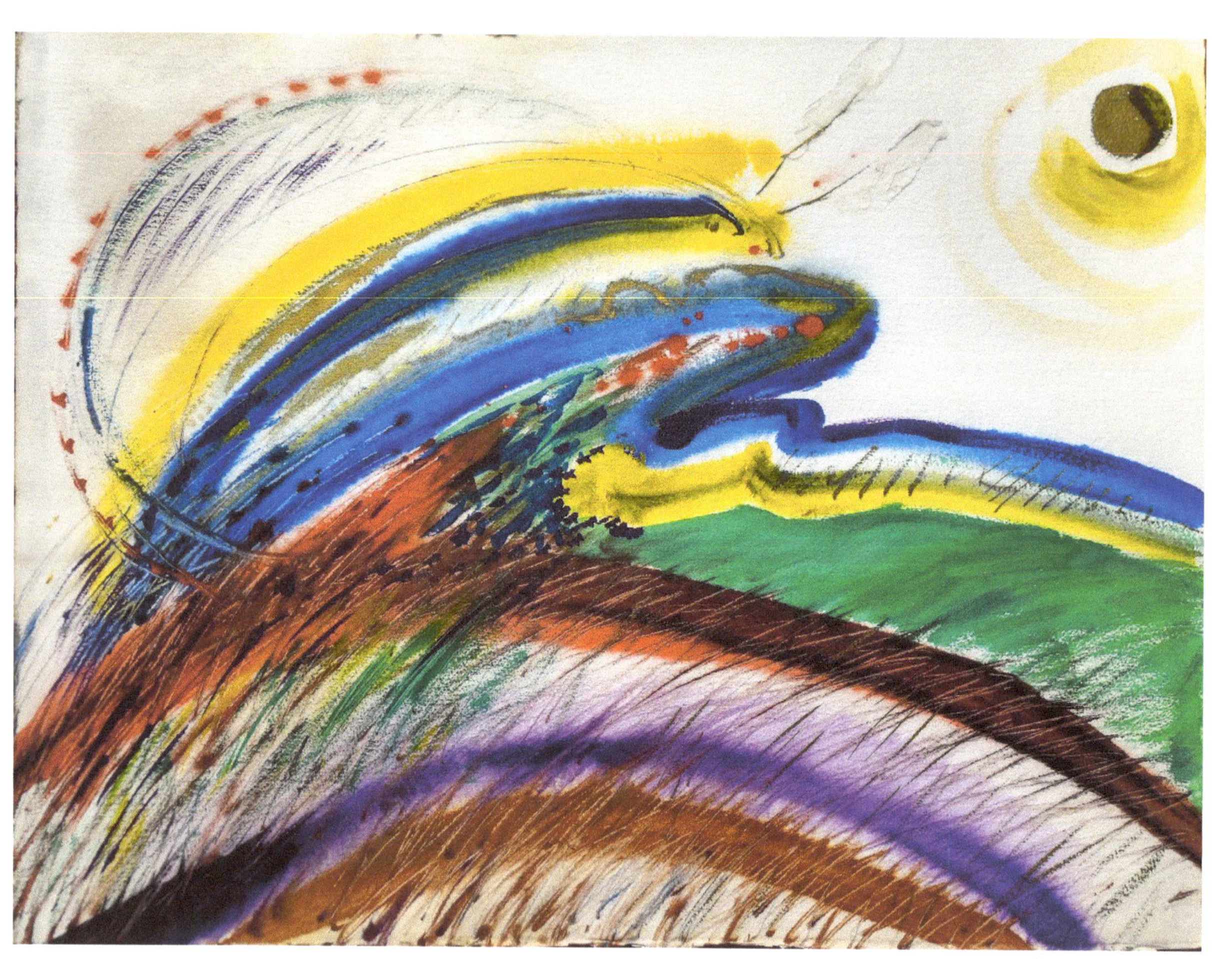

Time to Write

I am an impatient toddler
unable to sit still to write
too busy living

Playing, rearranging the toys in my house
digging in the yard
watering plants, repotting,
nudging sunflowers to grow

Other days hiking with friends
sometimes talking,
better still, stretches of silence,
falling behind the others,
indulging in the crunch of the trail,
catching the sudden scent of blossoms

I drift to other times
to dreams
awake or dreaming
does it matter

At home
spreading an old sheet on the back lawn
stretching and rolling like a puppy
happy as I've ever been
Is this nirvana?
Is it as simple as this?

Whiteflower, my new last name,
expanding into the whole me
as earthy, as hippy, as free-spirited
as I've ever wanted to be

So for now,
too full of savoring my yard, my solitude,
the earthworm I disturb who undulates
back into the dirt

Can I say?
This is why I'm not finding the time
to write?

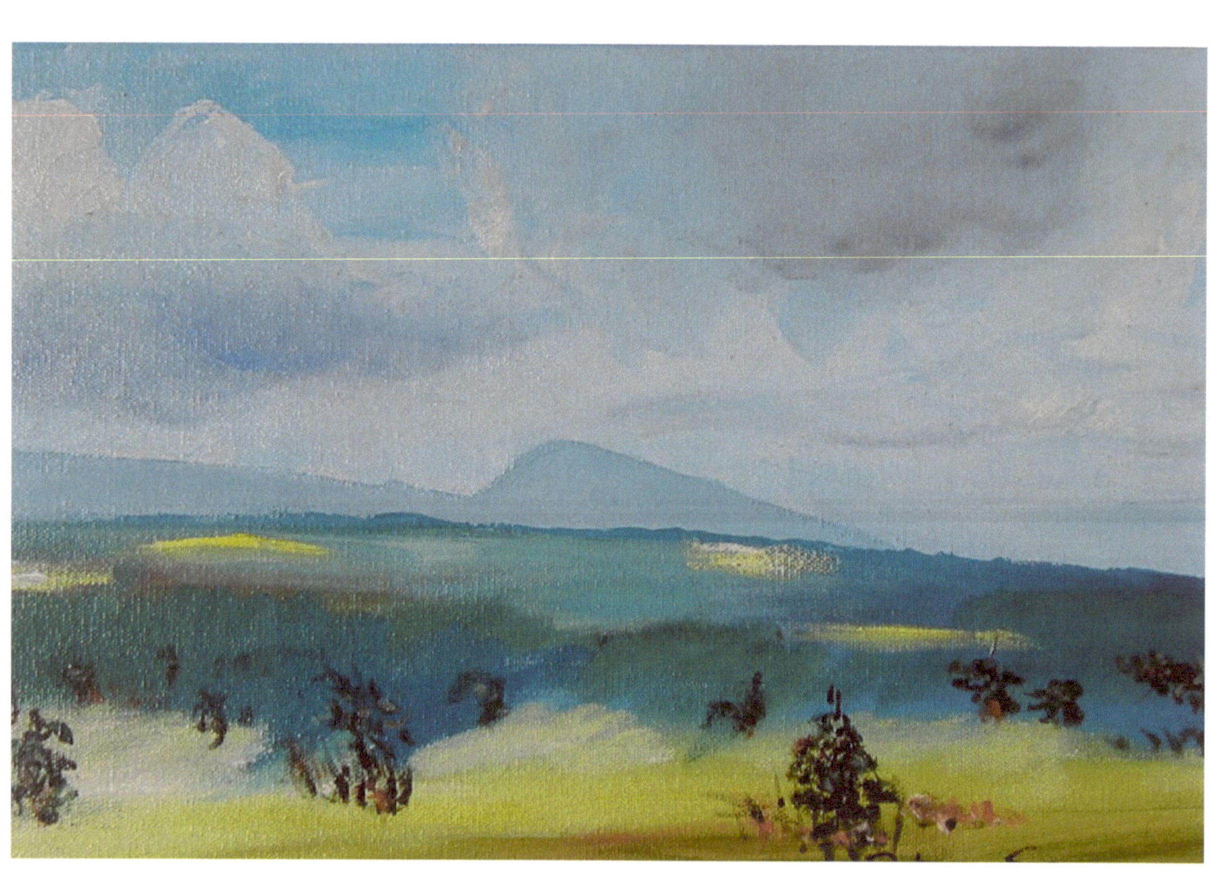

There is a Stillness Here

There is a stillness here at the edge of the crater
A silence that rings in my head
in spite of the wind in the grasses,
bird chirps, the distant highway,
the shift of leaves high in the ʻohiʻa

Stillness
in the barely moving clouds,
in the rock face,
the now-frozen lava,
the steady sun on the gravel edge

Stillness in the stark white against black
of the tropic bird

Koa'e kea
sailing through the vast space
of Kilauea Crater

The stillness
calling to a deeper silence
dropping in
to the vertigo of it all
releasing
the deep
inner call

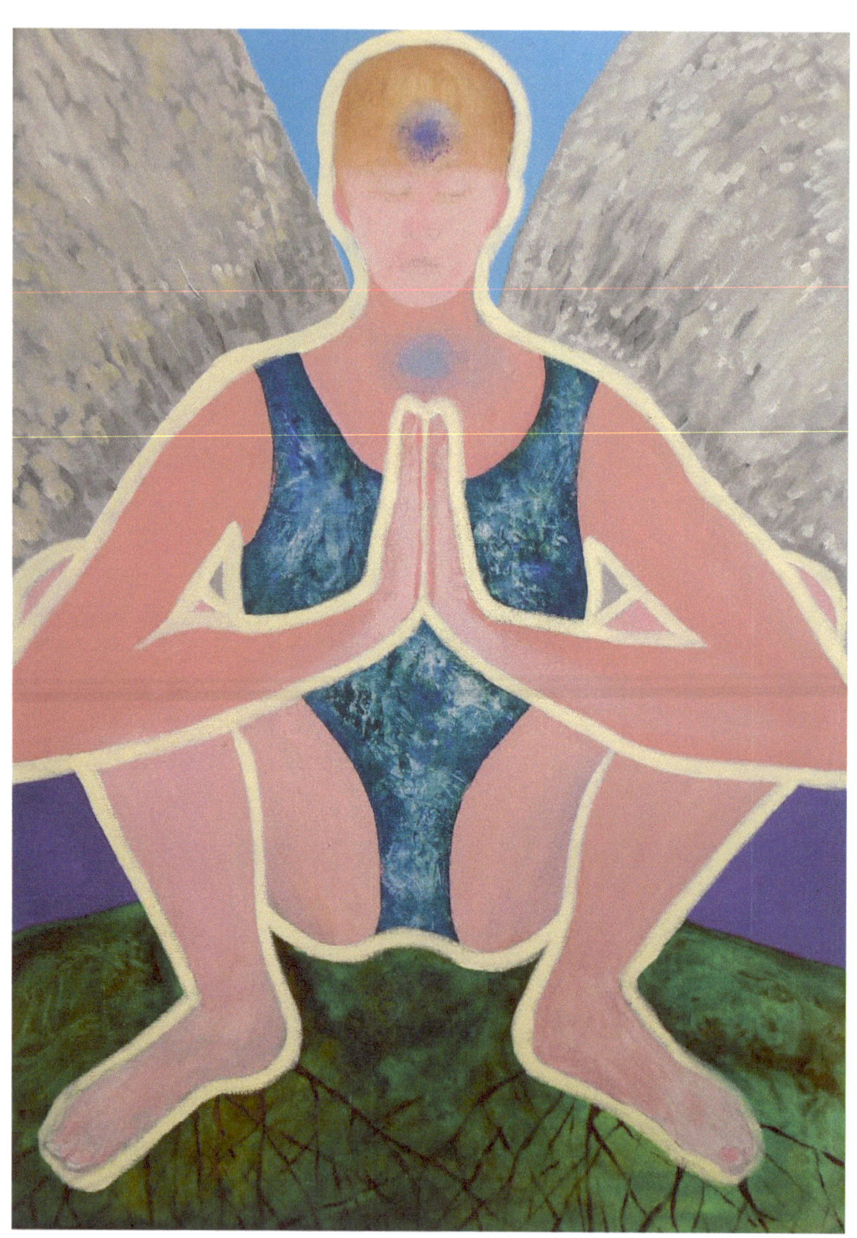

Santosha

There was a time when I desired
to have someone to share all this

a stunning day,
a favorite crater hike,

but today
contentment
total

through yoga study
learning Santosha/ inner contentment
can be a choice

today
grateful
for that choice
no need more

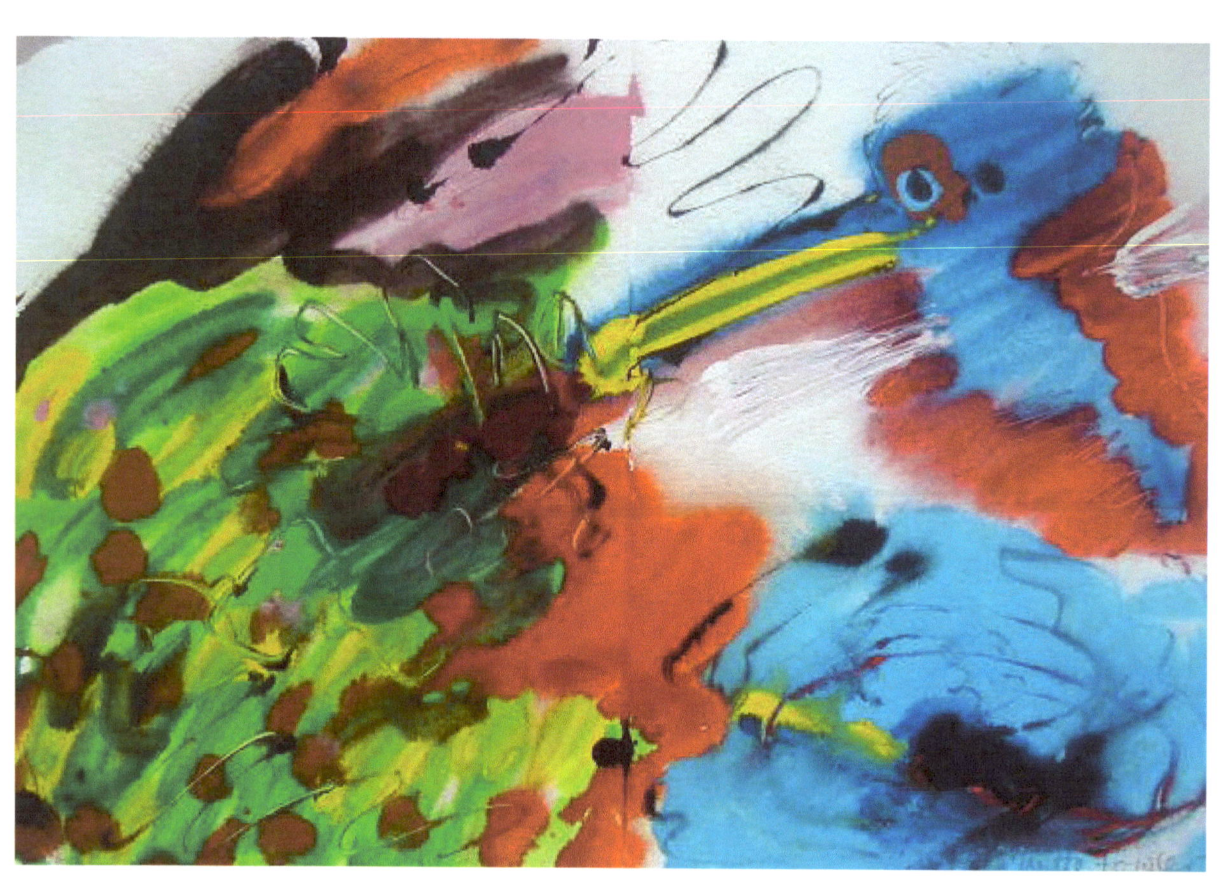

Just Before Waking

Just before waking
a vision
nearly one hundred ʻapapane
gathered on a grassy lawn

In an instant they lift up, swirling,
a moving mandala
of red and black and flickering white

I could never have imagined
so many of these vibrant,
ever-singing, ever-flying
birds of this island rainforest
in one place together

To see them rise at once
in my inner sight,
a flying, moving vortex of color

Ahh,
a pre-wakefulness flash
a gift

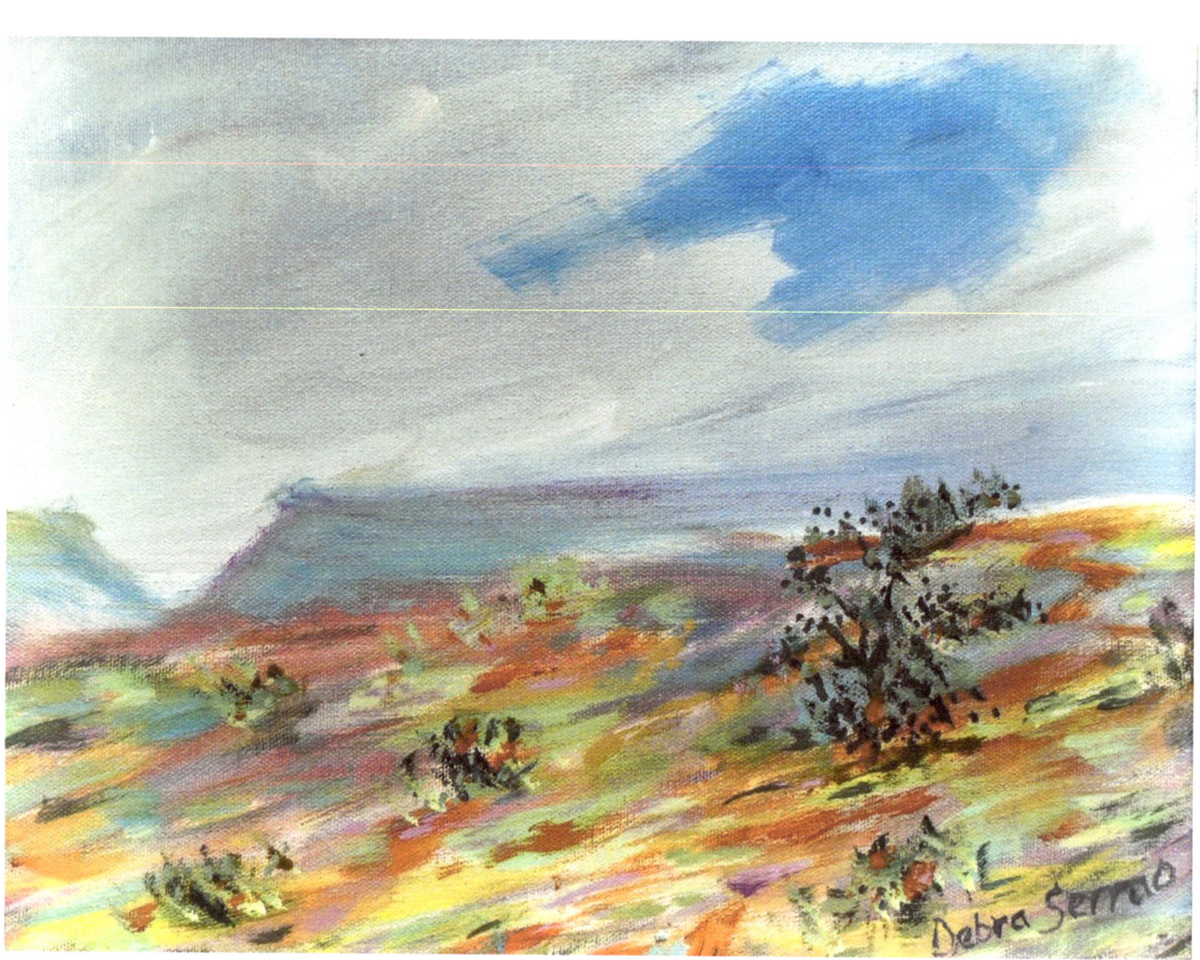
Debra Serrao

I Go Down to the Crater's Edge

She says
sit awhile
and hear the
buzz of silence
between your ears

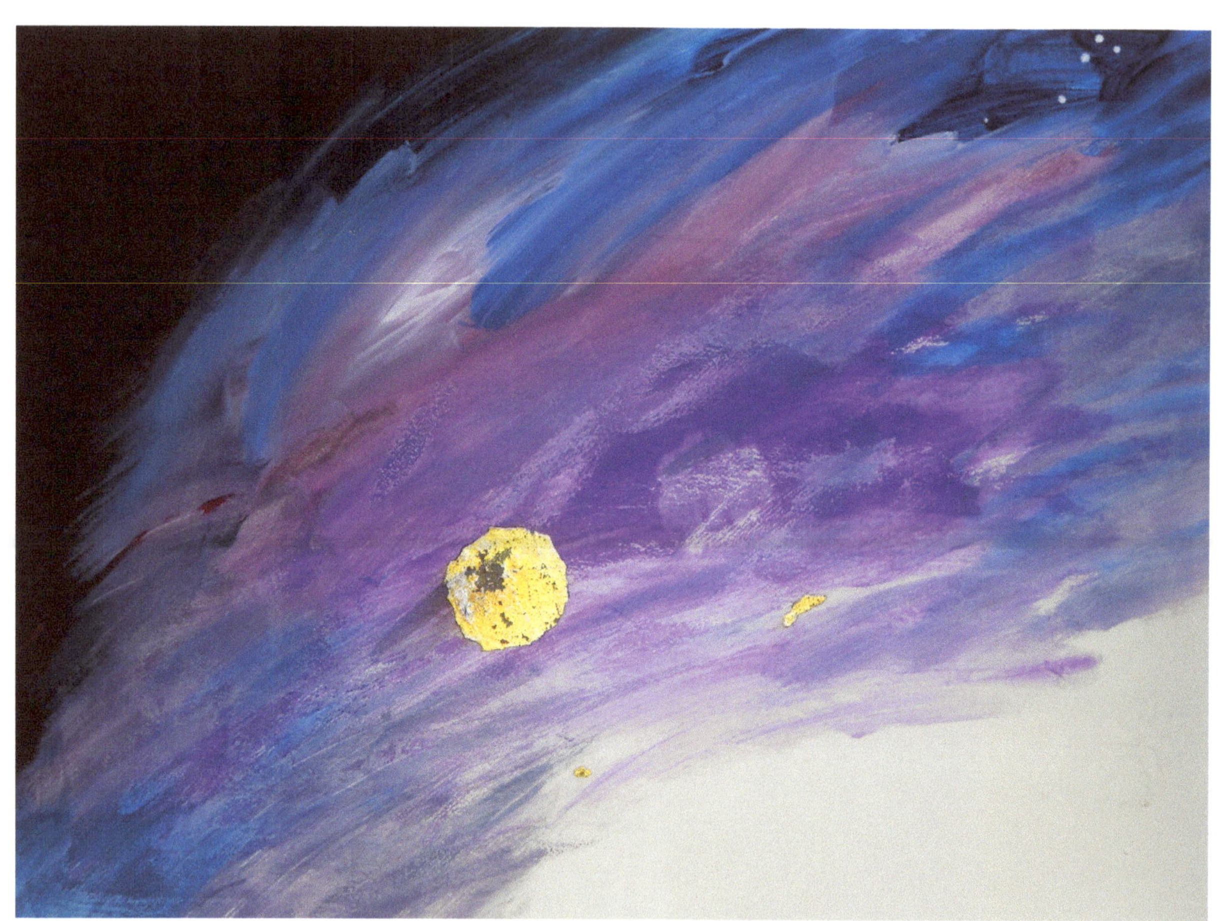

Can I Look

Can I look
at whatever comes to me
in the eye
without fear
with wonder
with deep peace
I wonder

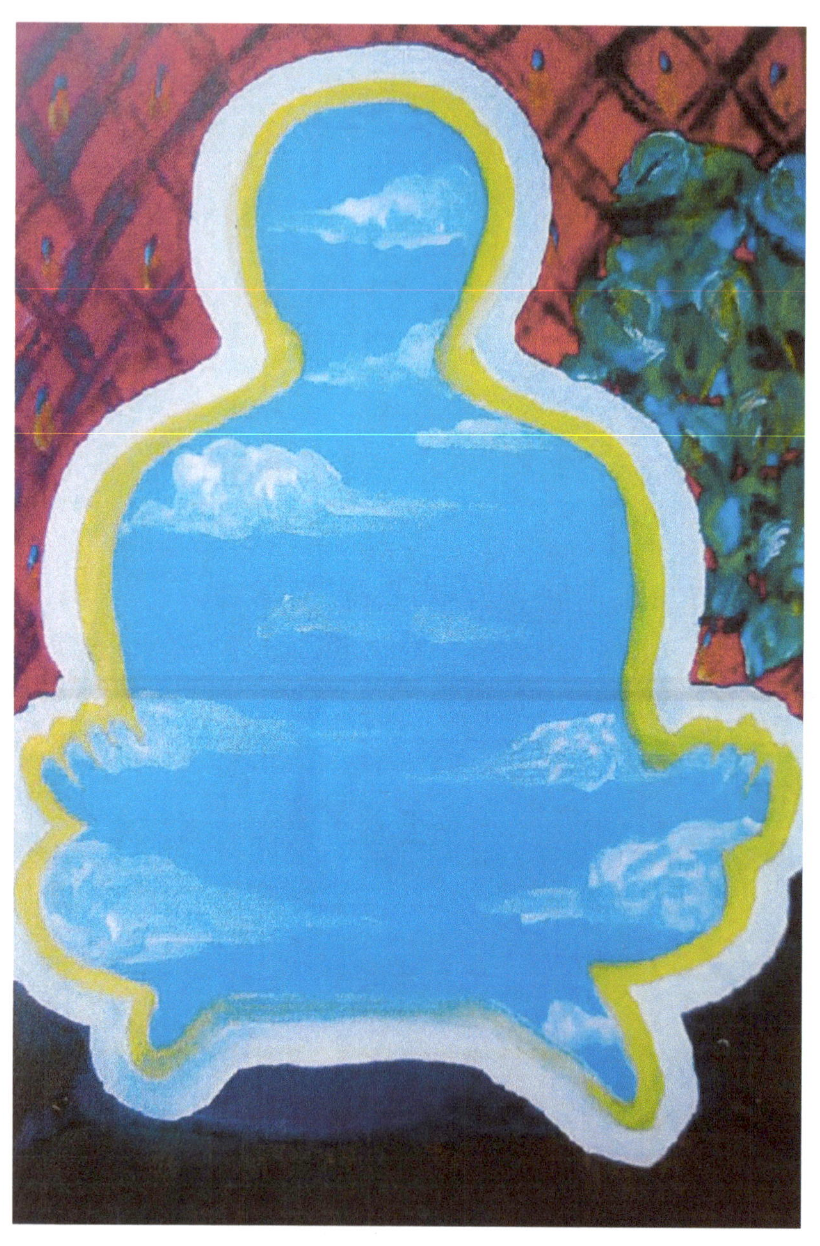

What is My Focus, Anyway?

When I haven't written for weeks
I think I'm a person who can no longer write

If I am
Is that so bad?

Busy
My head, my heart, have been busy

Can I be OK being one
who isn't writing?

Cultivating peace of mind
has been my focus
I guess it's taken up the space for writing
for now

The question is, do I want to feel bad about that?

What's my focus, anyway?
Is there anything more important than peace of mind?

And what IS peace of mind
If not allowing what is
to be what is.

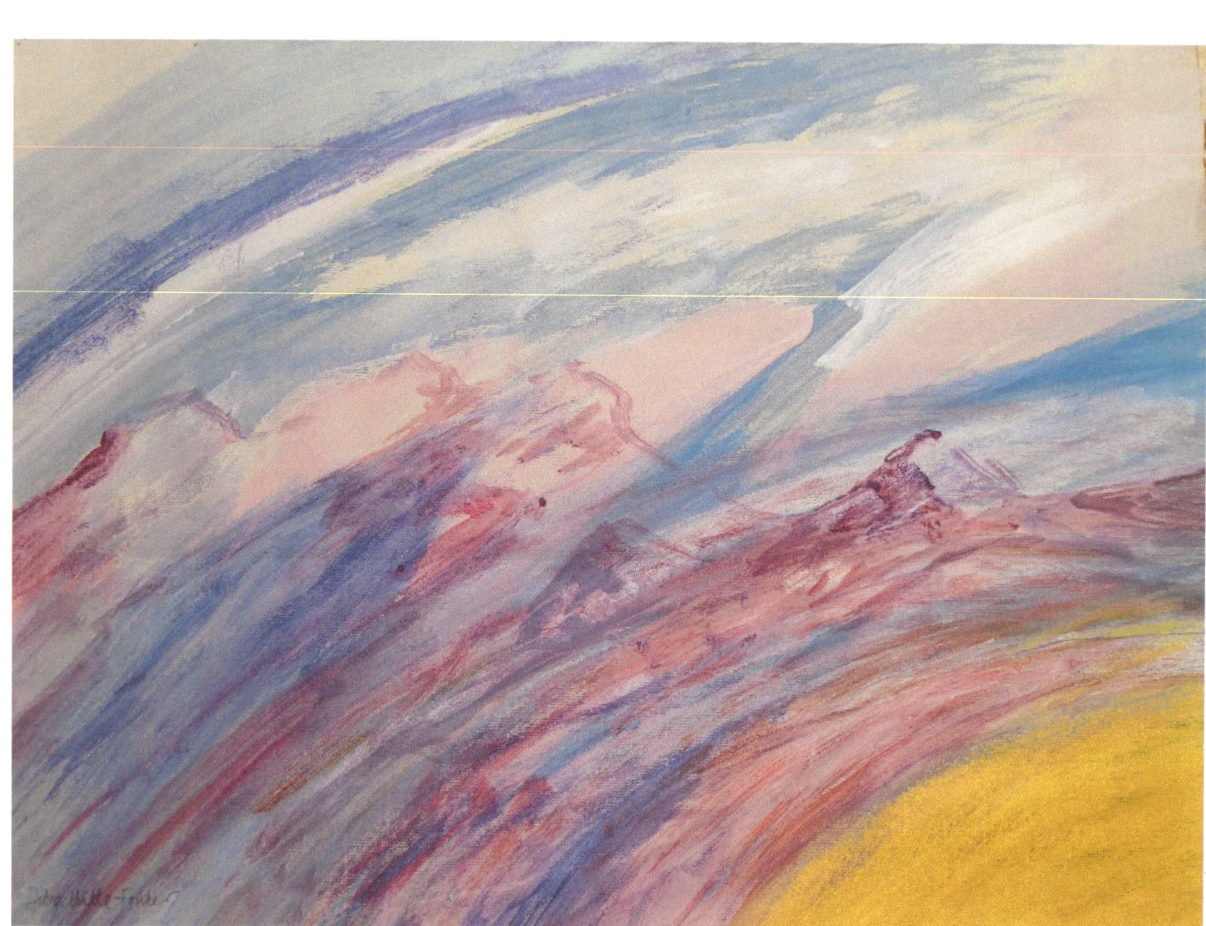

Let Me Be

Let me be
a prayer flag
blowing in the wind

Blast me with storms
and sun
whatever it takes

Release all the prayers that ever were
and ever will be

Loosen my threads
bleach me, let me fade
while the thousand and one true prayers
scatter like healing ash

Seek out the homeless, the heartless
all the faces and souls I hurry through on facebook
too much suffering,
too much unkindness

Let me be a prayer flag
Release the longing
the one, true prayer
. . . May all beings be happy

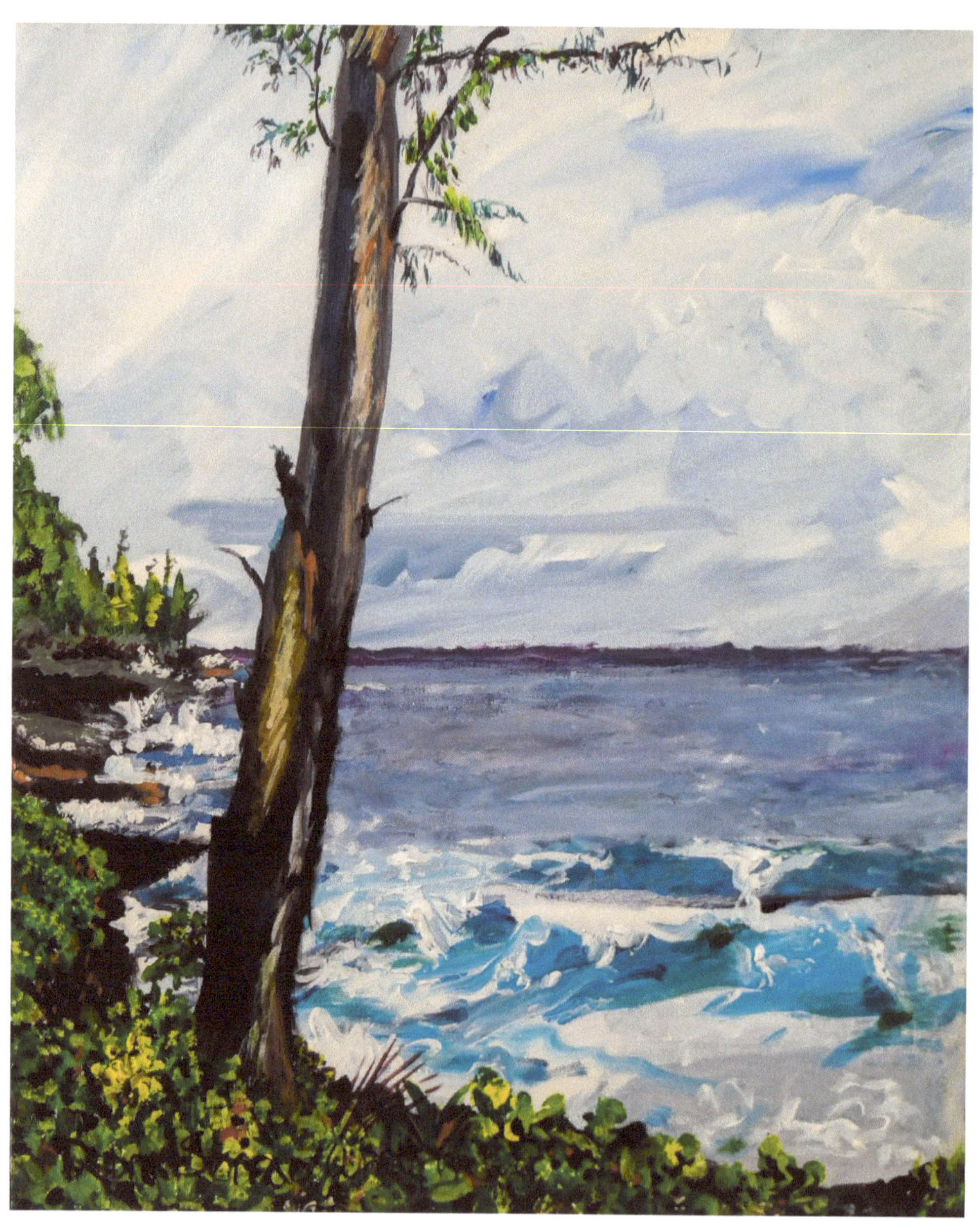

With deep gratitude
to
all my sister-writers, teachers
and guides
through the years.

May All Beings Be Happy